Rhyme Time for Rugrats.

Catherine Anne Monsour

BookLeaf Publishing

Presentation by *BookLeaf Publishing*

Web: www.bookleafpub.com

E-mail: info@bookleafpub.com

ISBN:9789358314731

First edition 2024

DEDICATION

To my first readers, children - and theirs.

PREFACE

Dear Reader:

One simple wish - to share with children (and others) the sheer delight and sometimes power of words, to use them to express emotions, to paint pictures - to communicate. And a hope that this little book may do this in a small way.

Anne.

Next Door Cat

Next Door Cat didn't come today.
I wonder why he stayed away?
Was it something that I said
When I chased him off my bed?
Did I frown at all the hair
He left clinging to my chair?
Perhaps I seemed a little tense,
When he jumped up on the kitchen bench,
Seized my sausage, ran off with it?
Well, yes, I yelled - a tiny bit.
But I didn't mean then to offend
My furry, fussy, feline friend -
There's only one thing left to say:
I'm sad the cat stayed away today…

The King and Queen Say No
(For Oscar)

In the land of Odd lived Princess Pearl,
A very lucky little girl.
The people loved her quite a lot,
So whatever she wanted, the princess got.
She said, "I'd like a silken gown,"
And they found her the silkiest gown in town.
She said, "I'd like some silver shoes,"
And they brought her a hundred from which to
choose.
She said, "I'd like a snow-white horse,"
And they answered, "A horse? Yes, yes, of
course!"
She said, "And a unicorn for a pet?"
Now this was difficult to get,
For unicorns are hard to find,
But no one ever seemed to mind.
She said, "I'd like one red hen, two cockatoos,
Three little pigs, four kangaroos
And five white mice. That's all for today."
They said, "Yes, Your Highness, yes, yes, right
away."
Now life in Odd was sweet and free
While Pearl got what she wanted immediately,
But one day this came to a sudden stop,

When the princess said, "I want a lollipop."
The King, her dad, said, " No, dear, we
Are just about to have our Royal Tea,"
And the Queen, her mother, gently said,
"No lollipop, darling, time for tea instead."
"NO?? They're saying NO to me?!
I want a lollipop, I don't want tea!
I want, I want, I want...I...I..." -
And Princess Pearl began to cry.
The tears that fell from her dark brown eyes
Were of a truly enormous size.
The Queen said, "Please don't cry, my pet,
I fear our feet are getting wet."
But cry she did, and the water rose
And covered the King's and Queen's royal toes.
Before long, things began to float
In the palace halls and the flooded moat,
While Pearl went on crying, her wide eyes
brimming,
And things in the palace started swimming.
The palace lamps were all extinguished,
And how that soaking King and Queen wished
Their daughter would stop her dreadful bawling!
But still those big tears kept on falling,
Until next morning - or so one hears -
The princess, at last, ran out of tears.
Pearl was sorry and sad, her heart was sore:
She said, "No one loves me anymore!"
But her parents said, "We love you still,

We always have and we always will.
But here is something you have to know:
One of the ways that parents show
They love you is by sometimes - saying no!"
The sun came out, and dried the water,
And the King and Queen, and Pearl, their
daughter,
Went downtown to the Candy Shop
And bought the biggest lollipop
You could ever wish for or hope to see,
Which they shared together, after tea.
And the people cheered like anything
For their majesties, the Queen and King.
There were special cheers for their Princess
Pearl,
A very lucky little girl,
Who smiled again because now she knew
Parents sometimes say no, but they still love
you.

In Honour of Lord Sandwich

There is nothing in the language
That exactly rhymes with sandwich -
But when tums are growling to be fed,
Two slices of delicious bread,
With something in between,
Is just the thing
For a lord or king
Or a hungry Queen!!

A Poem About Pigs

*Mother Pig told her children, " Now you're all
quite grown,
It's time for each of you to have a house to call
your own."
So the three brother pigs set out next day,
Each to build his house in his own special way.*

*Pig One found straw, and said, "Just what I
need!
This will make a very fine house indeed!"
He built his house quickly – because he wanted
to sing
And play his guitar, his favourite thing.
The house was soon finished: it didn't take long,
Then he strummed his guitar and sang this song.
"Oh, I've built me a house of straw!
I'm glad the work's all done,
I can sing my song the whole day long -
Now it's time for fun!"*

*The second brother pig was a dreamy sort of pig,
Sleeping was his favorite thing.
He quickly put together a little house,
With sticks and bits of string.*

He didn't really care that the house wasn't strong,
He curled up on cushions and sang a sleepy song.
"Oh - I've built me - a house of sticks,
And now -the work's - all done,
I'll sit and sleep - and sleeeep some more,
In the warm, (snore) warm (snore) sun."
(SNORE!)

The third pig didn't use straw or sticks:
He built his house with - you guessed it --bricks!
He worked very hard all through that day,
Never once stopping to sleep or play.
And soon his house stood strong and tall,
He'd built it so it wouldn't fall.
And when the Wolf came into town,
He blew the others' houses down,
The two little pigs then had to flee
To the fine, strong house of Pig Number Three!
The wolf came and huffed and puffed with all his might -
He could have huffed and puffed all night -
But the house didn't crumble, and he slinked away
Without his dinner. And, do you know, they
All learned a lesson that's easy to tell:
When you do something – always do it well!

Very silly Verse

Barnaby Brown rode into town,
Bought ten apple pies, and when
He'd eaten each pie,
He said, "I don't think I
Could eat another ten,
But I'd like to try
So please may I
Have ten more pies?" And then
He ate until
He felt quite ill,
And said, "Won't do that again!"

Penelope Pink always liked to drink
While sitting on a mat.
That's not polite?
It's quite all right,
That's perfect manners – for a cat.

Rodney Red likes to stand on his head.
He said, "It's a marvelous feeling,
With my feet in the air
And the floor in my hair,
And a wonderful view of the ceiling!"

Sebastian Gray tried every way,

To teach his pig to sing,
A nice idea,
But it's quite clear,
A pretty impossible thing.
So then he taught
His pig to snort
In tune to his violin.
(Sometimes it's wise
To compromise –
And everyone can win).

The Insect

Pretty little flying thing,
Do you bite? Or do you sting?
Does your beauty fine conceal
Something I'd not like to feel?
Here I stand, and wonder why
You can flutter, flit and fly,
While I am grounded,
And confounded –
Just - wondering.

Please, Tommy Jones, Get Out of Bed!

"Wake up! Wake up!", the Teddy Bear said.
"Hey, Tommy Jones, get out of bed!
The clock says it's now FIVE minutes to eight.
Come on, Sleepyhead, it's getting late!"
But the little boy, in slumber deep,
Just gently snored and stayed asleep.
And sixty seconds on the clock
Passed by, tick tock, tick tock, tick tock...

The Teddy Bear said, "Now it's FOUR to eight.
Come on, get up, the weather's great!
The sun is bright, the sky is blue:
There are hundreds of out-of-bed things to do!"
But Tommy Jones, with eyes tight closed,
Just dreamed a dreamy dream and dozed.
Another minute on the clock
Passed by, tick tock, tick tock, tick tock...

The Teddy Bear then, a little mad,
Said, "Tommy Jones, this is too bad!
We bears don't like to get irate,
But now it's just THREE minutes to eight!"
It scowled and growled and shook its head,
While Tommy Jones dreamed on in bed.

Another minute on the clock passed by,
Tick tock, tick tock, tick tock.

Teddy Bear said, "This isn't right!
I know you've been asleep all night.
It isn't fair, this will not do -
The minutes left now number TWO!"
It gave the bed a little shake -
But Tommy Jones still didn't wake.
Another minute on the clock
Passed by, tick tock, tick tock, tick tock.

Teddy Bear said, "I cannot wait!
The time is now ONE minute to eight.
We bears don't like to make a fuss,
And nothing much ever bothers us -
BUT, my friend, this must be said:
You really should GET OUT OF BED!!!"
And then...
BRRRRRIIINNNNGGGGGGGG...
A tingling, jingling, jangling shock!
The alarm bell rang -
It was eight o'clock!!!!

And Tommy Jones woke straight away,
And said, " Another awesome day!"
Then the little boy jumped out of bed -
And tucked his bear in there instead.

"Tick tock, tick tock, tick tock tick tock,"
Softly sang the bedroom clock.
Time passed, of course, but the teddy bear
Was fast asleep, and didn't care...

The Music Man

A music man came to our town,
He said his name was Bunthorne Brown.
His shoes were old but very clean:
His coat was purple, striped with green.
The people gathered every day,
When Bunthorne Brown began to play.
And when he played his violin,
The cats and dogs and pigs joined in.
And when he played his blue guitar,
The cows sang, "MOO!" and the sheep sang,
"BAA!".
And when he played his silver flute,
The ducks sang "QUAACK!" and the owls sang,
"HOOT!".
And when he played his old banjo,
His tambourine or his piccolo,
Everyone called, "Encore! Encore!" –
Which simply means, "Again! Play more!"
But when Bunthorne played his new saxophone,
Suddenly – he was all alone.
The sound was wrong, too sharp, too flat,
"It hurts our ears! We can't have that!"
The people said, as they walked away.
"We're very sorry, but we can't stay!"

*Bunthorne thought – and thought – and then he
knew
Exactly what he had to do.
He went inside, and closed the door,
And didn't come out for a month or more.
You know what he did there, all alone?
He learned to play that saxophone!
Yes, he practised, practised night and day,
Until at last we heard him say,
"By George, I've got it! Yes, yes, yes!"
At last, he had achieved success.
The sound was now so sweet and clear
That everyone came out to hear,
And marvel at the mellow tone
Of Bunthorne's golden saxophone!
And Bunthorne Brown slept well that night,
Because he worked hard - and got it right!*

A Strange Happening

At twilight, magic filled the air,
And freaky music, from nowhere,
Followed me down a darkened lane:
Just where I was, I can't explain.
But the moon was blue, the sky was green,
When I found myself somewhere I'd never been.
It was a long, long way away -
Where animals had things to say!

There was Simon, a soup-sipping stork,
Who stopped sipping and started to talk.
He said, "With a spoon, it's all eaten too soon,
So I always sip soup with a fork!"
Then Ronald, a purple-ish rabbit,
Said, "I'm sorry, I have a bad habit.
When I see anyone with a cake or a bun,
Well, I just have to reach out and grab it."
And then Gabby, a giggling goose,
Told me, "I'm glad that I'm not a moose!
I'm happy instead of antlers on my head,
I have feathers, much neater and spruce!"
Next thing, a whale called Wayne,
Said, "There's something I'd like to explain.
I'm afraid I will get a bad cold if I'm wet...
Never swim in the rain!"

Then I spotted a little fruit fly,
She looked as though she might cry.
She said, "Why are folks rude, If I land on their
food?
They always say, 'Shoo!' – never 'Hi!'"
And, sadly, I couldn't say why…
and so…
I left that place that I can't explain,
And walked back up the secret lane.
The music had stopped, the magic gone,
It was night now, the streetlights shone.
This was the Real World that I knew,
Where animals never speak, or do
Un-animal things: but - I'll go back there, when
There is Magic in the air again.

The Fly (For Hugo)

Andi Pi taught a fly how to dance and sing,
It learned to tap, to waltz and rap,
And do the Highland Fling.
Andi Pi said to the fly, "I think you could go far!
Kid, stick with me, and you will see,
I'll make of you a Star!"
And the fly said back to Pi, "That sounds good
to me,
But it's not the norm
For flies to perform:
Better get yourself a flea."

The Search

Our Nanni lost her spectacles:
She calls them "specs" for short.
Now Nanni's mostly cool and calm,
But right then she was distraught.
"I had them here a while ago,
When I had a cup of tea.
Now I can't find my specs at all!
Wherever can they be?"
Paul said, "Don't be upset,
We'll find your specs for you."
"Oh, thank you!" said our Nanni,
"Because I don't know what to do!"
Poor thing, she was in a pickle,
And we love to help our Nan,
So that is how The Great Search For
The Missing Spectacles began.

Paul looked on the table, I looked on the chair,
We both looked in the bread bin, but the specs
weren't there.
We looked in cupboards, we searched the floor,
Beneath all the pillows, behind the door,
On top of the bedpost, under the bed,
Above the bench, in the garden shed.
In the oven, on the rug,

Inside her favorite coffee mug -
In the bathtub, in the sink,
Behind the couch - then we stopped to think.
We'd searched for the spectacles everywhere,
Except –
Except in Nan's grey curly hair. We looked and
yes, the specs were there.

So Nan had her specs, and she could see,
And, to thank us, made scones for morning tea.
"But next time my specs are lost," she said,
"The first place you should look, dears, is on my
head!"

The Stickybeak

The strange Stickybeak has two very sharp ears,
And one thin, rather pointy, long nose.
Its hair is a fright, and it looks quite a sight,
As it runs on the tips of its toes.
It will sidle and sneak, it will pry, peer and peep,
So be careful when it is about –
Because if there's a secret that you want to keep,
That Stickybeak's bound to find out!
And then it will tattle, and we all know now
that'll
Mean you have a secret no more!
So please take this advice,
Don't think about it twice!
Show that strange Stickybeak out the door!

The Genie

I found an old and rusty lamp,
And rubbed till it was gleaming:
To my surprise before my eyes
There stood a genie, beaming.
"What do you wish?" the Genie said,
"Abradabra kazamkazoo!"
(Which roughly meant, it seemed to me,
" I can make your dreams come true!")
He winked and blinked and smiled and said,
"Now, do you wish for treasure?
Chests all filled with gold and pearls,
Wealth beyond all measure?"
That sounded good, that sounded fine,
I told the Genie so.
All those riches could be mine?
And the Genie bowed down low.
And said, "Abracadabra kazamkazoh."
But then I had a sudden thought,
And it was plain to me,
That wealth alone won't make this world
A better place to be…
What we really needed now
Was quarrels all to cease.
I said ,"Genie, here's our greatest wish –
A world that nurture's peace."

The Genie slowly shook his head.
"That's one thing I can't do.
But when people all learn to agree,
That wish will, then, come true!"
He grinned and winked and blinked again,
And then, just as I feared,
He bowed and twirled around three times,
And quickly disappeared.

And I was left there all alone,
No diamonds, pearls, or gold,
No treasure had he left to me,
But the thing that I'd been told -
That I have now passed on to you…
Abradabra kazam kazoo!

The Writer

Why do I do this? Why put myself through this
Thoroughly bothersome pain?
I search my mind ceaselessly but words won't
come to me:
They just tease and torment my brain.
I'd rather wash dishes, or polish the floor,
Cut my toenails, or repair the screen door,
Than fight this battle with words that just might
Turn into a poem I'm trying to write.
So this is the end. It's time for me
To stop this writing and set my mind free:
I'll put down the pen!! - and then, and then -
(SIGH) I'll only pick it up again:
For after all is said and done,
Writing is frustrating, irritating, aggravating,
Exasperating, bothersome fun.

Grammar

What's happening with grammar?
We've been using it for years.
But now there's something going on
That's painful to my ears!
You say you swum across the river?
You're bringing me to tears…
You didn't swum, you swam across –
But - now you HAVE swum, my dears!

Yes, English can be troublesome,
But don't despair and bin it -
There are certain writings to be read,
Utterances that have been said,
That could only be said or read -
In it.

3am

THEN
Big hand on twelve, small hand on three,
Babby drinking peacefully.
Toddler peeps in, wide awake,
Not a sound does small child make.
Shining eyes, cheeky grin,
Climbs aboard, snuggles in.
Suddenly, fleetingly,
The world and all its treasures belong to me.

NOW
The digital clock is saying three,
Not the way it used to be.
Now I struggle out of bed,
Eyes are bleary, nose is red,
There's something that I have to do,.
But I won't be skipping to the loo!
My legs don't work. Back feels broken,
Bit put out by being woken.
Mirror tells me not quite yet dead,
But there's hay, not hair, upon my head.

Tiresome these things may be,
When now the clock is showing three,
But they fade beside the memory

Of a time when the world was mine.

Time

Time is progress, time is money,
To waste a second is a crime.
In this instant world we live in
All we have to save is time.
Pre-sliced bread and TV dinners.
Packaged food, no need to wait,
Instant people in a hurry,
Worry that they'll be too late.
Machines do dishes, clean the floors,
Washing, drying, micro-waving:
Press a button, no more chores,
Think of all the time we're saving...
Computers click and meters tick,
Time makes dollars, time makes cents:
Yesterday is gone forever,
Tomorrow soon is past tense!
Seconds flying, catch that walk sign,
Run run run, you'll miss your bus -
Fasterfaster fasterfaster fasterfaster- faaaaast...
Hey! What's happening to us?
Time!

Friends

What is it I want,
Wish for, in the end?
To be worthy of those
Who call me friend:
To never hurt,
Though I have and I do,
The ones I love dearly,
Those dear, dear few.
I pray they'll forgive me.
Can you?

The Age of Reason

I woke one wondrous day at dawn,
To sights that pleased my eyes.
It seemed that, with the day new born,
The world had grown wise.
The howling hounds of war that prowled
The Earth, with hate and spite,
Had vanished as the glowing ball
Of sun banished the night.
Fish swam in unpolluted seas,
Birds flew in endless skies.
There were only happy greetings,
No heart-breaking goodbyes.
The poor were dressed in robes of silk,
And dined on finest fare,
With sage and poet, bishop, king,
While Earth's song filled the air.
All creatures sang together,
The sweet, melodious tune,
And that wondrous silver morning
Became golden afternoon.
Then I woke again, this time
To cold reality,
But I was not sad, for I'd seen
Just how things will be,
When we turn the page

And reach the Age of Reason.

Lights

In the spotlight, that's where our pulses race!
In the spotlight, it's like no other place:
When that bright light hits us, we forget all toil
and care -
We're entertainers, there's an audience out there!
Behind the footlights, that's where we belong
When together we sing our favorite song:
Though we miss a cue, forget a line, skip three
pages - it's still fine,
The show will carry on, while the stage lights
shine!

The play is ended, the stage lights fade and die.
Final curtain means time to say goodbye.
The props, the costumes, will be all packed
away,
The stage will be set for yet another play -
Other players, and a very different scene.
It might seem that we have never ever been -
But the lights that once were yours and mine
Will spring to life again - and shine.

Procrastination

Procrastination will only lead to sorrow:
If you don't do today things you can leave until
tomorrow,
Things won't get done, they'll not even be begun,
Do it now.
Procrastination will get you simply nowhere,
If there's somewhere you must go, then step
along and go there.
Don't stay to count the cost, he who hesitates is
lost,
Do do it now.

If you stop to mull things over, very soon you'll
find
The race already ended, and you've been left
behind.
We've been told that we should always look
before we leap,
So take a look, by all means, just a little peep,
but do it now!

Procrastination is for the mild and meek,
If something must be done, don't leave it till next
week.
Time marches by, how the seconds fly!

So take that step, move along, don't care how,
Do your thing, sing your song, do it now.

If you know you want to do it,
And you don't you'll surely rue it -
Life is short, do what you ought to do… now.